Here's what people are saying about *Loving Your Long-Distance Relationship* by Stephen Blake...

Just a note to let you know that your book is probably saving my relationship with the most wonderful girl I know. Thanks, from both of us.
- *Paco, Miami, USA.*

I loved reading your book! Do you know that I started crying once I began reading your introduction.? It described my emotions to a "T".
- *Mayra, California, USA.*

Loved this book! Was so helpful for me in my long-distance relationship, which, by the way, I was absolutely convinced would NOT work until after reading the book. - *Jane, Colorado, USA.*

What a wonderful idea and inspiration your book is to me. - *Cody, Alberta, Canada*

Thank you for writing this book. You have done a great service for a great number of very lonely people. - *Karrie, New York, USA.*

Congratulations on inspiring so many people to keep trying. - *Samantha, Sydney, Australia.*

Reading the introduction to your book was like reading my life story..I finally feel understood and -- yes -- encouraged! - *Robin, New York, USA.*

Here's what people are saying about *Loving Your Long-Distance Relationship by Stephen Blake*...

I love your book. Thanks to your book you have made me realize that I am not alone. It sounds like you have helped many people. - *Daniel, Washington, USA.*

Thank you so much for your book - it has been heaven-sent! Can't wait for the next edition.
- *Karen, Toronto, Canada.*

I wanted to tell you how much I appreciated your book. Reading your book helped me feel better as well as give me hope. Thank you! - *Toni, Alberta, Canada.*

I couldn't believe my eyes when I found this book on the shelf!! I started reading and couldn't put it down! Now I've passed it on to my boyfriend.This book has been a real help...now I don't feel like the only one on planet earth who is feeling some of these things. - *Colleen, BC, Canada.*

Thank you so much for sharing your experiences! It is so reassuring to know that there are people going through the same thing that I am going through.
- *Katherine, Virgina, USA*

Thank you for writing such a helpful book. Your book has been very comforting. Once again thank you. - *Adrienne, Ontario, Canada.*

*L*oving *Your* *Long-Distance* *Relationship* *for Women*

Kimberli Bryan

with forward by
Stephen Blake

Anton
Anton Publishing Inc. * Canada

Published by
Anton Publishing Inc.
305 Madison Ave.
Suite 1166
New York, New York 10165

Cover art by: Sterling Shanski.

Printed in Canada.

ISBN 09680971-6-2

There are so many people that help to shape our lives and make us who we are, in one way or another, that when an opportunity arises to thank them, it's almost impossible to do so. How do we even begin to thank people for something so profound as helping to make us who we are? I can only hope that those who've touched my heart feel that connection as strongly as I do.

I want to thank Stephen for giving me the opportunity to write this book in the first place. He saw something in my work that made him think I could do it, and I am so glad he was willing to put his faith and his company behind me, even back when I was still just a voice on the phone to him.

My heartfelt gratitude goes out to those friends and family members who have trusted me with the personal details of their relationships and let me analyze and take them apart until I understood how they work. Without that practice, I would have faltered on my path long ago.

Deepest of all is the gratitude I feel for my husband, Gary. Without his love, my life would be barren in ways too painful to contemplate. Babybear… I gonna love you forever.

Kimberli Bryan

Contents

Foreward

From the moment I finished *Loving Your Long-Distance Relationship*, I knew that I would not feel complete until a book was written by a woman, for women. Although I did my best to empathize with my girlfriend's thoughts and feelings at the time I was writing *Loving*, I realized that I could never appreciate the intensity and uniqueness of the experience from her perspective. In *Loving Your Long-Distance Relationship for Women*, Kimberli Bryan has done just that. Surpassing my expectations of what *Loving for Women* should be, she has complimented my insights by showing how the experience is parallel, yet different for women in many respects.

Kimberli's assertion that only solid relationships last regardless of distance, captures the essence of why some long-distance relationships work and why some do not. She writes that distance is merely another "pressure" or "test" in a relationship, and that only those bonds based on mutual respect, commitment, and communication can survive periodic stresses that challenge all couples. I couldn't agree more. After receiving thousands of letters from couples across the world, it has become apparent that it's not the distance or the length of time that separates two people that determines the outcome of their future, but how committed both are to seeing things through the good times and the bad. Relationships built on solid foundations endure distance. Those formed on weaker grounds do not.

I think the most important part of a woman's experience in a long-distance relationship that tends to be overlooked by "us males," is the need for emotional communication and empathy. Whereas males put more of a premium on physical encounters (or the lack, thereof, in a LDR), women see physical intimacy as an extension of a process by which a man shares himself emotionally with his mate, and at the same time tries his best to empathize with her feelings and experiences. In a long-distance relationship, men need to understand how to share their feelings openly and honestly, while at the same time assuring their partner that they understand what the other is going through. A good example of this is Kimberli's portrayal of an emotional airport goodbye, where her husband was more concerned about "fixing the situation" instead of communicating that he was feeling just as badly as she was, for leaving.

Another theme that permeates *Loving for Women* is the need for couples to realize that men and women are different, and that for a relationship to last, both must accept, understand, manage, and actually appreciate those differences, rather than treat them as obstacles. Kimberli sites examples such as going out dancing, flirting, and having platonic friendships with the opposite sex as areas that can easily be misinterpreted by a couple if they do not understand that men and woman may perceive the same situation in completely different ways. She maintains that if these situations are understood and managed, they will not threaten a relationship, and can actually be used to strengthen a bond between two people. Her consistent prescription of honest communication, empathy, and playful acceptance immediately turns perceived problems into opportunities for greater sharing and understanding between two people who must be apart.

Kimberli's message to women that "being in love and living apart forces two people to learn and express their needs, wants, desires, thoughts, and feelings to a degree that most people never do," should give women not only the security that their long-distance relationship can work, but that distance can actually strengthen their emotional connection to their loved one.

Without reservation, I now introduce *Loving Your Long-Distance Relationship for Women*: a collection of insights, feelings, and definitive coping strategies for any woman who wants to enrich her relationship. It will give you a greater understanding of yourself, your partner, and long-distance love, a unique experience that should be treasured rather than feared as a couple grows emotionally...together.

- Stephen Blake, author, *Loving Your Long-Distance Relationship* and *Still Loving Your Long-Distance Relationship*.

Introduction

O nce upon a time there was an ordinary woman who worked at an ordinary software company. One day in the hall she met a prince disguised as an ordinary man, and she knew almost immediately that he was The One.

He looked at her and decided that she must certainly be a princess, for only a princess could steal a man's heart with a single smile. In truth, she'd never been a princess before and never thought to become one, but in loving her, he crowned her the princess of his heart, and even in her grandest dreams she'd never imagined anything so perfectly wonderful as that.

They were thrilled to have found each other... but soon the prince was forced to leave his princess and travel to another land, where he lived without her for more than a year. It was the longest year of their lives. They were rarely together, and then only briefly. Their hearts broke and they went mad with loneliness for each other. Each of them, knowing the true beauty of the other, was sure that the other was doubtless besieged with irresistable offers of love and passion, every single day. Neither thought themselves worthy to hold the other's heart...

especially from such a distance. They suffered mightily and cried copiously… until a miracle began to happen. As time passed, they each saw that the other continued to wait and continued to suffer, with love. The princess began to trust that he really loved and wanted only her, and would settle for no other. The prince came to believe that she loved him so much that she would wait… no matter how long he was away.

And so they did wait, for one another. Time passed slowly, but their hearts rested more easily in the sure and certain knowledge that one day they would be together, forever.

When that day finally came, there was feasting and dancing in all the kingdom. The family and friends who'd comforted the two when they were suffering alone came to rejoice with them and celebrate their joy at being together again, at last. The prince and his princess joined their hands and vowed before all to love each other forever and ever.

And they loved happily ever after.

When I met Gary and fell in love with him, I had no idea what I was letting myself in for. At that time he was a software engineer, and in the computer industry two years is about the normal life span of a job for good technical people. There's so much demand for their talents that they change jobs with some frequency to jump up their salaries, and they usually travel... a lot.

Within a few months of our meeting, he was living in Denver and I was still home in Austin, missing him and feeling profoundly sorry for myself. For one-and-a-half long, lonely years, we saw each other twice a month, in Austin or Denver... and we lived for those weekends.

There were no books on surviving this sort of thing at that time, and no one either of us knew had ever made it work. But we loved each other too much not to try. We had some of the best times of our lives on those weekends together... and some of the worst times between them. He buried himself in hard work to stifle the pain of our separation, but no amount of work could relieve the suffering. Three times I reached my breaking point and ended the relationship. Three times within days, I was back on the phone with him, crying my heart out. It was hell.

After the longest eighteen months in the history of the world, he came home to Austin, we got engaged, and everything was as wonderful as we always knew it could be. We were busy planning our wedding and being a normal couple. We were both happier than we'd ever been. He was offered an opportunity to work in Switzerland and we were thrilled about it. We arrived in Switzerland and moved into our new house a month after the wedding. I thought our separations were behind us and I was ready for happily ever after.

I was sadly mistaken.

For the next two years, Gary traveled all week, every week. Although he was home on weekends, I spent five days a week in a small village in a foreign country where I had exactly one friend and could barely speak the language. I have never felt so alone.

And that's how I came to know a thing or two about long-distance relationships. Since then, I have met countless people who are living with them: people who travel for business, people in the military or in love with someone who is, people who are away at school, and so many people who have fallen in love over the Internet and are living for the day they can join their mates in one country or the other. This book is for them. I am touched by their stories because I know what it's like to wait and wish and want so much that nothing else matters.

If you're in a long-distance relationship, welcome to the fold. It is my most heartfelt wish that what you find between the covers of this book gives you comfort, makes you laugh, helps you solve a problem or two, and most of all, gives you the sure and certain knowledge that *You Are Not Alone*.

Can This Relationship Survive?

If you take away the distance factor what you're left with is a normal relationship ... The absolute requirements of a good relationship are respect, commitment, and communication. If your relationship has those three qualities going for it, you'll survive anything.

♡♡♡

That's the big question, the one that haunts you late at night in your too big, too cold, and, certainly, too lonely bed. You've seen your friends' relationships crash and burn - some, even when they seemed perfectly suited to each other - and you can't help wondering what chance your relationship has to survive, especially given the distance between the two of you.

And then there's *The Way Men Are*. You know what I mean. No one, except maybe you, really believes that he can be that far away from you for that long and resist all temptation. Some of your friends, and maybe your mother, are kind enough not to say it, but you can still feel them wondering why you trust him so much… and puzzling over when it was that you became so naïve. The sheer weight of their combined opinions is enough to make you doubt yourself and your faith in him. So you lie awake at night and think that maybe it's really stupid to trust him. If you think about it long enough, you'll start wondering if you really do trust him, or if you just want to so badly that you've resorted to lying to yourself and denying the obvious. This is generally the point at which you decide to break it off with him - and this time, you mean it! Or maybe you'll just cry yourself to sleep, again.

If this sounds painfully familiar, it's probably because you're a perfectly normal woman in love with a man who's living somewhere else, and not really the crazy person you feel like you've become. Despite all the long-distance relationships that don't make it, you'll be happy to know that some do. It *is* possible to get from where you are now to happily ever after. This book is intended to help you navigate that path as painlessly as possible.

♡♡♡

Only Good Relationships Tolerate Pressure.
First, the ground rules: I will tell you the truth, even
when it's ugly. I'm not writing a whole book of,
"Now, now, there, there… everything's going to be
all right." Telling you those things is the shared job
of your best friend, your mom, and your teddy bear.
I'm going to show you ways to evaluate your
relationship realistically, figure out what you need to
work on to strengthen it, and - once you've done that
- help you avoid the pitfalls and make the best of the
time you have to spend away from the man you love.

Brace yourself because we're going to start with
The Cold, Hard Truth. If you take away the distance
factor what you're left with is a normal relationship.
Some normal relationships make it and some don't.
There are various factors that can put pressure on a
relationship. A good, solid relationship can take a lot
of pressure before it cracks. Distance is one type of
pressure. Therefore, a good solid relationship is
likely to survive the pressure, and a weak one is
likely to crack. Build a strong relationship and not
only will it be able to take the pressure, but it will
endure more gracefully, which means less stress for
you and your love. Sounds good so far, right?

The absolute requirements of a good

relationship are respect, commitment, and communication. If your relationship has those three qualities going for it, you'll survive anything. If it doesn't, well then, at least you know what you need to work on.

Equality Equals Respect. Balance keeps the world on track and never more so than in relationships. Even with your girlfriends, you know that the friendship never works out long term if it isn't equal. If one of you likes the other a lot more, or one wants to spend a great deal more time together than does the other, that person feels neglected, the other feels annoyed, and the friendship falters. That's even more true in a romantic relationship. You must be partners, sharing equally in the joys, sorrows, and struggles of your life together, both wanting what you're building.

In friendship, you might sometimes be in a 'mentor' position, maybe with a younger friend, kind of helping her along and offering her advice when she gets into a situation with which you have some experience. Or maybe you've had a friend you really looked up to, who has helped you. In romantic relationships that can work, as long as it works both ways. If he's teaching you to appreciate the finer points of football as a spectator sport, that's great. But it won't work if he always has to be the one in control, unless, of course, you're the sort of person who enjoys being controlled. If he's also interested in having you teach him to rollerblade, then you have balance. His willingness to put himself in the position of student to you demonstrates his respect for you. If he thinks he can learn nothing from you, he doesn't respect you. You will not be able to tolerate that forever.

Most importantly, you must be the person you really are deep inside, when you're with him. If you've tried to become the woman you think he wants you to be in order to 'get' him, your relationship will fall apart as soon as you can't stand being that fake version of yourself any longer. Save yourself the pain and grief of that situation by being the person you really are, all the time. Then if a guy doesn't like who you are, he'll go away long before you care for him. That's a good thing. It's a mechanism for weeding out the kind of men that will eventually make you miserable anyway, so don't disable it by faking a different personality for his benefit. When you meet your soulmate, he'll love you for you and won't want to change a thing. Nothing feels better than that. It's what people mean when they use the phrase 'unconditional love'. It means he loves you -- warts, faults, character flaws, and all -- with all his heart.

Commitment. Frankly, it doesn't matter if your entire life revolves around making this relationship work if he's only semi-interested. An attitude of, "Let's give it a try," or, "Let's see how it goes," doesn't bode well for your chances. There will be problems, and if you're not committed to each other a problem becomes the signal to say goodbye.

If the two of you truly love each other and you know you want to be together no matter what, your chances are good. Talk about it, openly discuss the fact that there will be problems and times when you get hurt or angry or begin to wonder if the relationship is even worth it. Decide together, that no matter what happens, you will always talk about it and work it out, because being together is the most important thing to you. That kind of commitment is an excellent foundation for a stable relationship.

Make some ground rules. Maybe you'll agree never to go to bed angry, which will force you to stay on the phone until you get it worked out. The important thing is to decide beforehand how the two of you will handle it when problems occur, because they will crop up even in the very best of relationships.

The most difficult thing about not being there is, well, not being there. You can't run into his arms and make him listen to you. You can't hold him close and wait for the storm to pass. If he hangs up the phone angrily, you will be left sitting there, crying, wondering if it's over and if he's on his way to someone else for comfort. Don't put yourself in that position. Deciding beforehand that whenever you have a problem you'll talk it out, or that you'll each go for a walk and cool down then call back in a hour, will give you the security you need in order to keep that dreaded, long-distance panic at bay.

Communication. In romantic novels and movies, there is always some sort of 'misunderstanding' between the main characters that causes them to doubt each other, or break up, or turn to someone else. If they ever just sat down and had a nice, honest talk about their feelings and the situation they're in, the problems would instantly resolve themselves... and the movie would be over. That, of course, is why they don't do it. But then again, they're guaranteed a happy ending in two hours, no matter how badly they mess up. You aren't. Talk about the things that bother you while they're still small. Discuss molehills so that you don't have mountains to argue about later on. Remember that if the two of you can really talk to each other, and listen to each other, there is no problem you can't solve.

One day not too long ago, I walked into the house and Gary and I, out of the blue, had an exchange in which we each snapped at the other, rather pointlessly. I thought he was unfair to have lashed out at me for no reason, and he felt the same way. So there we were, each feeling wounded and resentful, all swelled up with righteous indignation over how we'd been treated.

About five minutes passed in total silence before one of us, and I honestly don't remember which of us it was since we tend to handle these things the same way, said, "I'm sorry I snapped at you. I think I'm annoyed about something else and just took it out on you." The other immediately apologized as well, and we sat down and talked for about an hour.

It turned out that we were both stressed about different things, he about work and me about a friend who had hurt my feelings, and we were edgy with each other as a result. Had we not discussed it right then and there, we would have gone away harboring hurt feelings and resentment that would be fed and compounded the next time something like that happened. Someday the cumulative total of all that hurt and resentment would have blown up into a huge battle that our relationship might not have survived. But because we discussed it and realized that what was really wrong had nothing to do with our relationship, it became a bonding experience that brought us closer. After we settled that disagreement, we went on to discuss the reasons we were stressed out. He was able to shed some light on my situation with my friend, and his insight helped me resolve the problem. I was able to bring a fresh perspective to his work dilemma and help him find the best way to handle it. So in one conversation, not only did we diffuse a potential area of trouble in our relationship, but we shared a deeply bonding experience and each helped the other solve a personal problem. That was an hour well spent, in so many ways, and serves as a prime example of what I mean when I say, handle the molehills and there won't ever be any mountains.

Assessing Your Relationship. If you've weighed your current relationship against these three criteria, you should have a pretty good idea what your chances are at this point. If you can clearly see that your relationship needs work, get busy. There is a lot of help to be found in bookstores and on the Internet. Couples counselors are available to work with you if you feel that you need it.

Once you have these important aspects of a good relationship in place, the two of you are ready to talk about how you're going to handle your separation and you're ready to set your boundaries.

Building a Solid Foundation

♡♡♡

Expressing your needs is a big part of the preparation for being apart. This is not the time to worry about what he'll think of you if you admit that you have an insecurity or two. He'll be flattered that you care enough and that you trust him enough to tell him... so do it.

♡♡♡

The ideal time to start building your solid foundation is before you separate... but it's not a requirement. You can choose to rework your arrangement at any point along the way. It's just a bit harder if you've already developed habitual patterns of behavior.

Ninety-nine percent of how happy a person is with a given situation is determined by how well it meets his or her expectations. If you hire someone to remodel your kitchen, the work takes two months, and your house is a disaster area during that time, you'll be happy with the work if two months of disaster was exactly what you expected. If the contractor led you to believe that he'd be finished in two weeks, you'll be furious before the work is done and you'll never hire that contractor again. It's the same work and the same contractor; the only difference is in what he led you to expect, up front.

Relationships are no different. If you and your mate discuss your feelings and worries honestly, you'll each know what to expect from the other as time goes on. If you tell him that you plan to go out with your girlfriends on Friday nights so that you don't sit home alone and feel sorry for yourself because he's gone, he won't be upset when a friend of his mentions seeing you in a club, and he won't misinterpret your actions and think you're on the prowl. If he tells you that it's hard for him to come home to a lonely apartment every night so he plans to work late often, you won't assume he's seeing someone else when he doesn't answer his home phone at 10 p.m.

These seem like simple situations that don't really need discussion, but life is different when you're a thousand miles apart. You can't see each other and be reassured by hugs and kisses and hungry glances. You feel lonely and vulnerable already, so it doesn't take as much to make you really paranoid. Expect raw feelings and you'll be able to better function as a couple, even when you're living single.

When Gary and I were first in the long-distance phase of our relationship, he didn't call me for an entire week. I was devastated. I thought that meant that our relationship was over. It turned out that he was having such a hard time with our separation that he just dove into his work, immersing himself, barely remembering to eat or sleep. He was coming home from the office so late that he didn't call for fear of waking me up. As if I would have minded being awakened when I'd just cried myself to sleep! But he didn't realize how it was affecting me; he was just dealing with his own pain as best he could. As soon as we talked and shared what we were each going through, the problem was solved, but it was one of the most horrible weeks of my life. You can spare yourselves that sort of thing by setting expectations. If I'd known he wasn't going to call for a week, I would have missed him, but I wouldn't have thought the silence meant more than it did.

Expressing your needs is a big part of the

preparation for being apart. This is not the time to worry about what he'll think of you if you admit that you have an insecurity or two. He'll be flattered that you care enough and that you trust him enough to tell him... so do it. If you need to hear his voice before you go to sleep, arrange a bedtime call, even if it's just for five minutes. If a five minute call is just a tease and you can't stand it, arrange to talk less frequently, but make them good, long calls. And shop around for a good calling plan; you don't need worries about the phone bill keeping you apart, too!

Most men seem to find it difficult to admit that they have insecurities and needs, so try to get him to talk to you about his. Look for clues in his conversation and behavior to the things that give him comfort. Most importantly of all, don't play games. Take all the advice you've ever heard about making men jealous and playing hard to get and all the rest and throw it out the nearest window. Be yourself and be honest. If he does the same, you'll be just fine. Keeping things together long-distance puts enough pressure on you both; don't make it any harder than it has to be.

One thing you absolutely must discuss is how long you expect to be apart. It might seem obvious if you're separating for a tour of duty in the military or if one of you is attending college for the next four years, but discuss it anyway, just to make sure you both have all the same information. Decide how you will handle it if the time gets extended for some reason, and under what circumstances you each think you should pull the plug on the whole plan. Just hearing him say that he'd chuck everything and come home if something really bad happened is strangely comforting, and those words will replay themselves in your mind late at night when you do most of your fretting, and they might just be the thing to soothe you to sleep.

At this time, the two of you also need to set some boundaries. Don't assume that everyone draws the line between what's okay and what's not okay in the same place. You'd be surprised to know that the world is full of completely rational people who don't agree with you on these fundamental issues. You aren't involved with all those people, so it doesn't matter what they think, but it does matter between you and your man.

The two of you need to discuss things that are pertinent to your circumstances. If you're going out with the girls on Friday night and plan to dance with other guys, make sure he knows it and is okay with that. Don't assume that he knows you will, of course, be dancing with other guys. He might not see that as the meaningless social activity that you do. If he doesn't, discuss it with him, explain how you feel about it, and consider a compromise if his feelings are strong on the subject. Don't make compromises that feel wrong to you, but negotiate an arrangement you can both live with. Talk about the kinds of situations you're each likely to face living in separate cities and functioning as single people that wouldn't be an issue if you were together every day, living as the couple you actually are.

Treat this subject seriously. You wouldn't believe the number of letters I get to my advice column from married couples arguing about what constitutes infidelity. Is cybersex cheating? Is flirtation okay? And just how far can he go at his friend's bachelor party before you will feel that he's being unfaithful? Is a lap dance cheating? The truth is that infidelity is defined by each couple. What's acceptable in your relationship might be a big no-no in someone else's... but the two of you have to define it for yourselves. Take the time to discuss it. You have to agree or you have to compromise; there are no other options that are healthy for your relationship.

Most importantly of all, listen to one another. It's not enough to just hear what he says. You must feel what he feels when he says it in order to truly understand him. If you don't get something the first time, ask him to rephrase it. Do this ten times if you need to, but don't move on to the next subject until you truly understand. Bumps in the conversational road are wonderful opportunities to learn more about each other, for only by explaining ourselves do we truly understand one another.

Communication is Critical

Sometimes the only difference between a possible strength and a potential weakness is in how you look at the situation. So stay open to the possibility of looking at things in different ways

We all have little things that really bother us more than it seems they should, things that provoke a reaction out of proportion to the event. For some women, it's when their mate looks a bit too hard at a passing babe or just naturally flirts with the waitress. For others, it's the fact that he seems more interested in spending time with his buddies than with the woman he loves. We don't want to be jealous about those things because it makes us feel petty and insecure when we most want to be cool. But we feel it, nonetheless.

If your relationship is going into the pressure cooker of long-distance circumstances, it's critical that you solve these small problems while they're still small. If you think he's a flirt when you're with him, what is your imagination going to have him doing when he's a thousand miles away? You don't need the torture of a lot of unexpressed insecurities. The two of you need to have a good, long talk -- preferably before the separation -- in which you both agree to bring up every little worry you have, no matter how small, and discuss them. He will mention things that you don't like, but you have to treat those things with as much respect as you want him to give your worries. If he's concerned about something silly, like the length of your skirts, or your best platonic guy friend, Joe, you can't just brush off those concerns because you know there's nothing to worry about. Ask him what you could do that would put his mind at ease, and then find a balance between the way things are and what he'd like to see that you can both live with. Don't hold out on principle, either. If you can give him what he wants without really compromising your values, just do it. That's a powerful way to show him how much you love him, and feeling that love will calm his worries more than anything else ever could.

Solving problems is a bit more difficult when

there is no obvious compromise. I used to worry about the fact that Gary always looked when a pretty woman walked by. He wasn't rude or embarrassing about it... but he looked. I said something about it one day -- not in an angry way, because I hadn't yet let it build up until I was upset -- and it led to an interesting conversation. He told me that there is something about the shape of a woman's body that is magnetic to the male eye. He said that if the average guy was lying mortally wounded in a hospital bed, and saw that shape in silhouette through a barely cracked eyelid, he would drag his nearly dead eye open to get a better look at it. I couldn't help laughing at the picture he painted. From that day on, it was just not an issue between us. Now if I see a pretty woman before he does, I'll nudge him and say, "Bra-less babe at 2 o'clock." He'll look and wink at me and I'll grin at him and then it's something we share, a sexy little game we play, rather than something he has to hide. Anything that the two of you share strengthens your relationship, just as anything that either of you has to hide weakens it. Sometimes the only difference between a possible strength and a potential weakness is in how you look at the situation. So stay open to the possibility of looking at things in different ways. Some of my girlfriends might think I'm crazy for pointing out pretty women to my husband on the street, but they all envy that easy, conspiratorial air we have between us as a result of sharing a sexy moment together.

Another really good way to get relief from that nervous, insecure feeling that comes from being apart is to find a phrase that means something special to the two of you, and use it often. In *Still Loving Your Long-Distance Relationship*, there was one letter from a couple who talked about their special phrase. Whenever he had to leave, he always told her, "I really love you... and you've got to believe that." It comforted her whenever he said it. Gary and I have always used a line from the movie, Zorro the Gay Blade. "I gonna love you forever." (Said with a sexy, fake Spanish accent, of course.) It's amazing how much a little thing like that can soothe an anxious heart. There is nothing more personal than the words you only say to each other.

Coping Strategies to Save Your Sanity

♡♡♡

One of the most quietly romantic things a couple can do is join their hearts in a special time and place. If you arrange to both go outside and look at the moon at the exact same time, you stand there, looking up, bathed in moonlight and thinking of him, while knowing that all those miles away, he, too, is bathed in moonlight and dreaming of you.

♡♡♡

You are physically separated by a ridiculous number of miles and there's nothing you can do about it. Your hearts, however, need never be apart. If you realize that in a bad relationship two people in the same room can both feel lonely, you'll see that physical proximity has nothing necessarily to do with feeling close and feeling loved. All you have to do is find other ways to help foster that feeling of intimacy between you and your mate.

Phone Calls. The phone is still the next best thing to being there. Hearing that voice on the other end of the line is a very physical sensation and the responses are immediate. It's still preferred, but it's expensive if you do it in the traditional way. Look for good calling plans, play phone companies off against each other, and switch plans as often as necessary to keep the best deal. Discuss your phone budget with your mate and be as generous as possible with this indulgence. It'll do more for you than anything else.

♡♡♡

The Internet. If the two of you have computers, you're in for a rich experience. There are just so many ways to take advantage of the Internet to communicate with your love. Obviously, there's e-mail so you can exchange letters with each other all day long. And there are chat rooms and instant messaging systems like ICQ, which we'll discuss more in the last chapter. There are video systems you can use with your computer if you're so inclined, and software you can get which will enable you to use your computer like a phone and talk to your love at no charge, other than what you pay for your Internet account. You can send your mate virtual cards, flowers, postcards, erotic art, and vacations, most of them complete with music, and all at no charge. Those are easy ways to keep him feeling your love and knowing that you're thinking of him.

Packages. There is no limit to what you can send him… short of your own self. Send him those things that feel like love to you. It might be something as homey as chocolate chip cookies you've baked yourself, or as wicked as a pair of your panties and a picture of you in them. Things that are personal are best. Make a tape of songs that remind you of the two of you… and then duplicate it for him. Both of you listening to the same music is a bonding experience. Ask him to send you one of his big shirts with his cologne sprinkled on it. Then buy yourself a bottle of his cologne (or you'll never wash that shirt). Send him a bottle of your scent, as well. The sense of smell is powerful and intimate, so stimulate it.

Tapes. Another surprisingly intimate thing to do is make tapes for each other. Consider getting yourselves a matching set of those mini-tape recorders that are marketed to executive types. They're quite inexpensive now, and the tapes are small so they won't cost much to mail, either. Carry the recorder around with you in your purse throughout the day. Whenever you think of something you'd say to him if he were there, just switch it on and talk to him. When you hear a song that reminds you of him, hold the machine to the speaker and record it for him, then whisper to him all the feelings that well up within you when you hear that song and think of him. I can promise you that he will never hear that song again without remembering what you said and feeling loved. Not only is the tape a quick and easy way to keep in touch with each other and to share every little thing, but it'll make you feel like he's as close as your purse, all the time. If you get some little earphones to match, you'll be able to put them on and listen to his voice any time you want or need to, and that might be just the comfort you need on those days when you miss him so much it hurts.

Letters. Handwritten letters are slow… but so very personal. Send them now and then, even if you are the queen of all technology, because there is something so moving about touching the letters formed by the hand of someone you love. Scent the letters with your perfume and kiss the paper with your lipstick. It might sound corny, but it got that way because people kept doing it, and people kept doing it because it makes them feel so close to one another. Besides, almost all the rituals of lovers are corny, so get used to it. You've just joined the ranks of the people who used to make you sick.

Journals. Another interesting option available to you is dual journals. Before the separation, or during your next visit together, buy a matching set of those blank page books and keep love journals. Each of you can record your thoughts and feelings throughout the day, much as you would if you were using the tape recorders. Each time you visit one another, in the last moments of your time together, switch journals. You'll both wave goodbye teary-eyed as ever, but you'll have clutched in your hot little hands a book containing days and nights of love and longing for you. That night, snuggled in your bed alone, you can read everything he wrote during your last separation while knowing all the while that he's doing the same. When you reach the end of what's written there, begin recording your own thoughts and feelings again, right where he left off. The next time you're together, switch journals again. Not only will you get through the separation more easily with those words to bolster your spirits, but when it's all over and you're living happily ever after, you'll have those two books as keepsakes. Who knows... you might even find special passages from them to read aloud at your wedding.

Photos. Pictures are powerful things. You know how often you look at the pictures you have of him. Don't you wish you had a hundred more? Send him pictures whenever you can. He will never tire of looking at them.

Gary and I bought a digital camera some time ago. It uses a floppy disk instead of film and saves the photos as graphic files. Now when he travels on business, he takes that camera and uses the timer to photograph himself in his hotel room when he arrives. He uses his laptop to send me an e-mail to let me know he's arrived safely and he attaches the picture. Meanwhile, I'm back at home thinking how quiet and empty the house seems. I get his note, open it, and there he is, in living color, smiling and waving at me. I can't even tell you how much better it makes me feel to be able to see him and picture where he is, and what it's like there. He can take pictures all day long, keep reusing the same floppy disk, just stopping to e-mail them to me whenever he gets a chance. Sometimes it almost feels like I'm there with him just because I see everything, too. Digital cameras are not inexpensive, but if it's an option, it's a wonderful thing for getting through those long, lonely days and nights.

Secret Rendezvous of the Heart. One of the most quietly romantic things a couple can do is join their hearts in a special time and place. If you arrange to both go outside and look at the moon at the exact same time, you stand there, looking up, bathed in moonlight and thinking of him, while knowing that all those miles away, he, too, is bathed in moonlight and dreaming of you. It's a profound thing because if you truly love someone and he truly loves you, you can feel each other across the miles at a time like that. Your spirits soar through the heavens and you embrace in front of the moon, and the warmth of that love envelops you like a blanket.

♡♡♡

Avoiding   Depression.   Long-distance relationships are not for the faint of heart or the weak-willed. They're difficult when they go smoothly and torturous when they don't. Sometimes the things that get to you seem so small and insignificant, yet leave you an emotional wreck for days.

The particulars of what will irritate you vary by individual. For me, it's the pictures. Gary has about a thousand photographs stored in shoeboxes that were all taken before we met. All the pictures taken since then are in photo albums around the house. I like the fact that he has all those old snapshots because they are such a good record of his life and it's fun to look through them with him. But one day when he was away on business, I went through one of the boxes looking for a particular photo, and I got incredibly depressed. All the ex-girlfriends, all the party pictures with women hanging all over him… it was just too much for me right then.

I did not see a single photograph that I hadn't seen before. But it was different somehow, when I was looking at them all alone and he was on the other side of the world. I told him about that when he got home and he offered to get rid of all the pictures that bothered me, but that wasn't the issue. The photos didn't upset me when I was with him, only when I was alone. So I learned not to go through those old photographs when he's away. It's a small coping mechanism, but it works.

That's the real essence of managing the situation. You have to look for the little things that get to you, the little things that hurt, and learn to work around them. Just as I advise recently broken-up friends to avoid the radio because for them every song will be a sad song, there are some experiences that will be inherently depressing for you when he is away. It's your responsibility to identify them and find a way to cope with them. If they're easily avoided, then avoid them. If you have no choice but to endure them, then find ways of looking at the experience in a less painful way.

I used to go to Gary's house to feed his two cats on my way home from work everyday. At first it was really hard. I'd see his house knowing it was empty, and I would feel so lonely for him. I'd go in, feed the cats, take in the mail, and get out of there quickly. Then I noticed how lonely the cats were and I felt bad for them. All three of us were missing the same guy and no one else understood how awful we felt.

They became my allies in misery. I made it my mission to make them feel like they weren't living in an empty house. On the way over to Gary's, I'd stop and pick up whatever I wanted for dinner. I'd go to his house, turn on the lights, turn on some music or the TV, feed the cats, and make dinner for myself. Then I might talk to a friend on the phone and generally just hang out for a couple of hours, petting the cats, and making noise. I did laundry there sometimes, I often left my car and took Gary's for the day, and I took the time to notice plants that needed watering. The result was that the cats were happier, his house was looked after, the car was better cared for because it was driven now and then, and I felt closer to him for being able to do all those things. His house was only empty when I left it that way. When I brought it to life, it gave me a lift in return. All I had to do was decide to make something good out of something bad. The simple truth is that most of life is that way. It's up to you what you make of it.

Having a Life When He's Away

♡♡♡

As tempting as it might be to live only for the times you and your mate can be together, it's quite unhealthy...you will become rather dull if you have nothing else going on in your life. To stop growing is to stagnate and stagnation is never pretty. This is the time to pursue those interests you've never had time for.

♡♡♡

You wave goodbye and suddenly your life seems as barren as the desert. You are alone, you have no life, you are pathetic.

Can you tell I've been there? Go ahead and admit it; when your man is home, you structure your life around spending time with him to such a degree that it does feel like you have nothing when he leaves. This is the time when you find out who your real friends are. Call your best friend, tell her you're sorry you've been out of touch for so long, and ask her what she's doing tonight. You need your friends in your life right now like you have never needed them before. Girlfriends can get bitchy about being blown off for a man, so be up front about the situation with all your friends. Tell them, "I really miss you guys when I don't see you for awhile, but he and I get to be together so rarely that I can't bear to miss a moment of it. Please forgive me for being so undependable right now, and I swear I'll do the same if it ever happens to you." All but the most cold-hearted woman will understand that.

You cannot afford to alienate your support system right now, so keep in mind what I told you before: ninety-nine percent of whether or not a person is happy with a set of circumstances has to do with how closely those circumstances match the person's expectations. If you want to be alone with your man, yet still keep your friends and family members happy, make sure they set their expectations of you realistically. If you've been spending three nights a week with your friends and your man is coming home for two weeks, tell them well before he gets there that you will miss them while he's home and you will look forward to seeing them after he leaves. They might pout a bit at first, but they'll accept that much more easily than they will accept you canceling plans you shouldn't have made in the first place.

Keep Your Life Full. As tempting as it might be to live only for the times you and your mate can be together, it's quite unhealthy. As we'll discuss in the next chapter, you will become rather dull if you have nothing else going on in your life. To stop growing is to stagnate and stagnation is never pretty. This is the time to pursue those interests you've never had time for. Fill the hours that you'd rather be with your man by taking classes, visiting friends, enjoying a hobby, or volunteering. If you've been dying to start your own business, do it now. Always wanted to try your hand at pottery? Now's the time. Thought about volunteering at your local animal shelter? Hey, those puppies aren't getting any younger. Being busy will save your sanity. When Gary and I were in our LDR, I had a very demanding job that I loved, and I was free to work as late as I wanted and really do it right. That job saved me from untold hours of depression and pacing the floor of my house. Had I not been so busy with something that meant a lot to me, I wonder if I would have been able to stick it out and wait for him. Not waiting would have been the biggest tragedy of my life.

Know Who Your Most Supportive Friends Are. At my bachelorette party, after we all got drunk and started telling each other how much we love each other, two of my friends apologized to me for things that they'd said about Gary while we were long distance. They both basically said the same thing: that he was having his cake and eating it, too. Meaning that while I was home, being faithful and living for his visits, no way was he doing the same. I wasn't mad at them because I understood that what they said reflected a lot more on the bad experiences in their own pasts than it did on Gary, or on my sanity for trusting him. But I also realized that the time Gary and I spent apart would have been easier on me if I hadn't been as close to those two friends as I was. Their words hurt and planted little seeds of doubt that I really didn't need at that time. Sometimes when I was having a down day, the things they said just haunted me.

Spend some time alone thinking about your friends and the kinds of people they really are. If you have a friend that adores your man and thinks he walks on water, that's the friend you need to visit on the days when you aren't sure you can survive another minute apart from him. She'll remind you of why you decided to wait for him in the first place.

My friend, Dorothy, saved me from despair more times than I can remember in just that way. She worked at the company where Gary and I met, so she knew him, saw what kind of man he was, and believed with all her heart that we belonged together. When it all got too hard and I felt myself starting to crack, I used to go into her office for a bagel and a pep talk. She never once, in all that time, expressed the slightest doubt in his love for me, or wavered in her sure and certain knowledge that we would make it through this time and live happily ever after. She was my safety net and I will always love her for that.

Save the cynical friends for those days when you're bulletproof. You know the days I mean: when you're so high, so crazy, so stupid in love that nothing can knock the smile off your face. Aren't those days just the best?

You might also want to consider having serious talks with the friends who are less supportive of your relationship than you'd like. Explain to them, tactfully, that the definition of a friend is someone who gives you an honest opinion and expresses all her misgivings right up until the decision is made. Once the choice is made, however, a true friend supports that decision no matter what it is. If you've committed to your long-distance relationship, a true friend will commit to it too, and help you every step of the way.

Getting the Attention You Need Without Straying. When you're living the carefree single life, you can flirt and date and generally get a lot of attention, so that you always feel attractive and desirable. When you're in a relationship, you trade most of that for the love of a good man who assures you of your desirability. In a LDR, you have all the restrictions of being in a relationship with very few of the perks, and it's easy to start feeling as though you're the only one who's getting no attention at all. I found this to be a problem because I'm a big flirt and I was used to a lot of attention. Then Gary and I got together and I was caught up in couple nirvana for a few months. When he later left to work out of state, I was in this strange limbo: no dating, no boyfriend, no nothing.

I found a couple of safe solutions to the problem. It helps if you have a good, platonic guy friend to go out with. I had two of them and got to go out and do things that looked like dates but were perfectly innocent and friendly, and that went a long way toward making me feel as though I still had a life. It's a good idea to make sure that your love meets the guy friend and likes him, so that he doesn't feel he has to worry about the friend's intentions toward you.

Another good solution is flirting in chat rooms on the Internet. They're perfectly safe because you're anonymous, and you can go in and flirt like a bandit, get lots of attention, and feel highly desirable. Then log off and go to bed a virtuous woman.

Be really honest with yourself and your man about your need for attention if it's causing you to feel badly. This goes back to the issue of discussing problems while they're small so that they never get a chance to become large. It's much better to flirt a bit and satisfy those desires that way, then to let them build up and risk making yourself vulnerable to another man you don't really want to be with, just because you need the attention.

Believing in Magic, Destiny, and Fate. Throughout history, the people who have endured tremendous hardship most gracefully and successfully were the ones who believed in something greater than themselves. The fact that these people were often fighting long, drawn-out religious wars should not deter you from applying the principle to your own situation.

We all tend to chalk things up to coincidence. It's easier for people to believe in the most outrageous series of chance occurrences than it is for most of us to believe that there could be any other explanation. But what you believe is up to you. If you choose to stop believing in coincidence as I have, then look at your relationship and see how incredibly unlikely it was to find each other among all the people in the world, now you can start to feel the magic of the possibility that your love is truly meant to be.

The best way to get to that feeling of destiny is to imagine, for a moment, that there are no coincidences and no accidents. Imagine that everything happens as it does because there is a plan. Look for evidence of that plan in your own life. Think about how you met, how you were both brought to that place at that time, and all the things that had to occur beforehand in each of your lives to get you both there. Then think about all the things that might have kept you from getting to know one another as you have. Yet none of those things happened. It's only when you stop dismissing miracles as coincidence that you find your destiny.

The certainty of your destiny will carry you swiftly and gently though some otherwise rough times, if you let it. We all have the option of choosing to see life as a mundane series of random events, or as a brilliantly woven tapestry of interconnected souls brought together in a particular way, at a particular time, to make magic.

Preparing For Your Time Together

♡♡♡

Change is threatening to most people and we tend to avoid what we fear. That fear is the single greatest danger to LDRs...change is the only constant in life; we must expect it, plan for it, and integrate it into our lives, as it comes.

♡♡♡

Another of the great challenges of LDRs is in the fact that people change continuously. When you and your mate are together you will tend to share most experiences, which makes it likely that you will grow together and in the same direction. By being apart so much, living almost completely separate lives, and having such radically different experiences, you risk moving in very different directions. If the two of you don't find ways to share those experiences intentionally, you risk finding yourselves growing apart some time down the road, without enough left in common to be the couple you once were.

I once saw an interview with Patrick Swayze that was done right after he'd made an emotionally demanding movie. He'd been married a really long time and the interviewer was asking him what prompted him to bring his wife with him to this remote country where he was filming the movie. I found his answer very interesting. He said that when he read the script, he realized that this experience was going to enrich and change him in profound ways, and he didn't want to do it without her. In other words, if he was going to grow and change so much he wanted to make sure that she had the opportunity to grow and change with him. When I heard that, I realized that it's no mystery that the two of them have been able to stay together and thrive in their marriage despite the pressures of fame and fortune and Hollywood, because they plan their lives together, deliberately, and they're smart about it.

Change is threatening to most people and we tend to avoid what we fear. That fear is the single greatest danger to LDRs, in my opinion. Change is the only constant in life; we must expect it, plan for it, and integrate it into our lives, as it comes. Do not wave goodbye to your man expecting that in four months when you see him next, that the two of you will pick up in this same spot, exactly as you are now. It will not happen. He will see things and do things between now and then that will change him, and so will you. You will both be altered by your experiences when next you meet. You can never step into the same river twice, because you have changed and the river has moved on.

The unknown is always a bit frightening. You can't know how he will be different, nor even how you will, but if you see it as the positive growth experience that it truly is, you can anticipate the changes with excitement and feed off one another. That's the best possible situation because it will allow you to grow twice as much as you otherwise would and yet stay perfectly suited to one another in the process.

Anticipating Changes in Him with Excitement Rather Than Dread. Talk, talk, and talk some more: on the phone, in e-mail, letters, and tapes, every chance you get. Take the time to share your experiences. Tell him about the little things that happen in your life and ask him about the little things in his. Share as much as you possibly can with one another and talk about what those things mean to each of you and to the life you're building together. Just because you are not physically standing by his side, doesn't mean you can't take him with you.

When he tells you about things he's seen and done, ask him how he felt about those things and pay attention to his answers. Try to feel what he felt so that you understand, as fully as possible, the experiences he's had. If you can feel what he felt, you can grow with him. By talking to him about it all and asking questions, you can help him verbalize his impressions. When he puts his experiences into words for you, he will gain a deeper level of understanding of what it all really means to him. So by getting him to talk, you not only share his experiences, but you enrich them for him.

Let yourself get excited about what's happening to him, the changes, the growth, the opportunities, because through him, they're your opportunities, too.

Planning a Few Surprises of Your Own. In the last chapter, I mentioned that the only alternative you have to growth is stagnation, and no one wants to see you stagnate. If you're the one off doing the traveling and living in a new place, growing is easy. But even if you are home waiting for his return, you have to find ways to expand your horizons. If he grows and you don't, you'll both have the perception that he's leaving you behind, and that's a breeding ground for insecurities that neither of you need.

The bookstores and libraries can be your best friends at this time. Find topics that interest you and read, read, read. Think about what you've read and discuss it with him. Grow intentionally. Take classes, do volunteer work, meet new people, and let yourself bloom. Invite personal development into your life and it will take you up on your offer. Do those things and every time you and your man come back together, you will have new aspects of yourself to share and compare. There is nothing better you can do for your relationship than to consciously grow as a person. Take the time to become the person you feel he deserves by being the best person you can be, and you'll both reap the rewards.

Dreaming and Planning, Dreaming and Planning. The Empire State Building began as an idea in someone's head. That's it, just a thought. It's so incredible to look at some monolithic structure or huge organization and to think that, at one time, it was just a thought that someone was pondering. The more the idea is mulled over, discussed, and dreamt about, the more energy is fed into it, and the better its chances become of maturing into reality.

Your relationship has the potential to go wherever you want to take it. Realize that your attention is a kind of energy. Spend time dreaming and thinking and talking about what you want, where you want to be in a year, three years, five years. Feed your dreams all the attention that you can, and they will come true. Don't sit around worrying and fretting about negative possibilities. That's just supplying energy to your worst nightmare. If you don't want it, don't feed it. Focus on your dreams, pour your energy into them, and encourage your man to do the same. If you both focus all that love and passion on building what you want together, it is impossible not to achieve it.

In life, there are certain things that are inevitable, things that when you look at them now, you realize that they just had to happen, eventually. Choose to see your relationship like that, and it cannot fail. If the two of you nurture that feeling of inevitability, the sure and certain knowledge that something this good was meant to be, then you will make it so.

Separating and Coming Together

You can't control how you feel, but you certainly have control over what you do about it. You are going to feel abandoned to some degree. There's no way around that because he is, in fact, leaving. But if you know this is coming, if you expect it and think it through beforehand, you have choices as to how to react to it.

♡♡♡

One of the biggest challenges we face in long-distance relationships is the emotional rollercoaster. When you are together, the joy can be so intense that your mood is absolutely euphoric, taking you to the highest peaks. Then when you part, the pain can be so crushing that you find valleys of misery deeper than you knew existed. If you can just understand why you feel what you feel when you feel it, it will go a long way toward calming the fear that you won't be able to survive it. We humans have an emotional self-preservation instinct that's no less powerful than the physical one. Any time a situation causes you enormous emotional pain, you are going to switch into survival mode and start trying to eliminate the source of that pain to save yourself. That's perfectly normal. The trick is being able to tell which kinds of pain truly constitute a threat to you, and which kinds are miserable, but worth enduring.

Why Do We Always Argue Just Before He Leaves? There is nothing more frustrating than spending the last days or hours of your time together arguing and saying stupid things that you bitterly regret the moment they're out of your mouth. Yet it happens every time, wasting precious moments and sending your man off feeling like he doesn't know if you'll make it together, instead of feeling loved and wanted and, oh, so happy to have you in his life, which is, of course, the way you want him to be feeling. So why does it happen?

You have to understand the difference between cognitive response and emotional response. Your rational, well-adjusted brain knows why he's leaving and that he hates going every bit as much as you hate to see him go. Your brain helped make the decision that being apart for this time is the right thing for both of you to do, and that it will be painful but it still needs to be done. Your brain knows he has no choice but to go, and that your separation is only temporary and that you both have very good reasons for being apart right now. In other words, your brain is fine with the whole situation.

Your brain, however, is not calling all the shots. The emotional response to the knowledge that he is about to leave is, quite naturally, a feeling of abandonment. Your heart is hurting because he's leaving you. Your heart is crying out in pain, "Stay with me, don't leave me. I need you to love me and hold me, comfort me and take care of me." And the harshest one of all, the Mr. Big of torturous emotional responses to a feeling of abandonment... "If You Really Loved Me, You Wouldn't Leave Me!"

Those feelings are powerful, and no matter how rational you are you can't help being affected by them. Needing him so much, and knowing he's going to leave you, can't help but make you feel rejected and unloved. Feeling that way when you love him so much can't help but make you angry. So before you know it, you're feeling anxious, then irritated, then maybe even downright mad. What kind of rat bastard would abandon the woman he loves to a world full of wolves and cruel bosses and rapists skulking around every dark corner? How could he? He must not love you. Certainly, he doesn't love you as much as you love him!

Knowing that's an irrational train of thought doesn't make it hurt one bit less. So you snap at him once or twice, which is usually followed by a full lashing out. Next thing you know, a big, stupid argument is born.

And then there you are, pressed against that huge plate glass window at the airport, waving pitifully with tears coursing down your cheeks, feeling like the worst shrew that ever walked the earth, hating yourself and thinking that if you were him you'd never want to see you again.

You can't control how you feel, but you certainly have control over what you do about it. You are going to feel abandoned to some degree. There's no way around that because he is, in fact, leaving. But if you know this is coming, if you expect it and think it through beforehand, you have choices as to how to react to it. What if, instead of letting those scary feelings make you anxious and then angry, you chose instead to just feel the sadness, and seek comfort for that? Going into his arms and cuddling and snuggling, feeling about four years old, is much more comforting to both of you and a far better way to spend your time than arguing.

Try to remember that the situation is the enemy, not him. He's every bit as battered and bruised by the situation as you are, whether, in his manly wisdom, he chooses to show it or not. Men tend to want to fix things. If he sees you hurting, he wants to make it all better, even if he's feeling exactly the same way. His natural response is going to be to say things like, "I'll be back before you know it," in an effort to make it all seem less horrible, and to put a positive spin on it. Men actually think that helps, even though you and I know that what we really want is to feel that he's just as miserable at the thought of being apart as we are. Keep in mind that you aren't hurting each other. The situation is hurting you both. But it won't last forever. In the end, the situation will be gone, and the two of you will be left standing together.

I Had Everything Just Where I Wanted It. So then he's gone for a long time, and you slowly adjust to it, never liking it or wanting it, but getting yourself into a routine so that you can still get things done and live a relatively productive life. You change a few things now and then, maybe reorder the contents of the drawers in the dresser, start separating the recyclables in a different way, or rearrange the furniture in your living room. It's all much better than the old way, of course, or you wouldn't have changed it, and everything's running smoothly, and you're proud of how well you're coping with being on your own again.

Now it's time for him to come home and you just can't wait to see him. You're so excited! You clean the whole house and buy something new and sexy to wear to the airport to pick him up. You bring him home, and hours later when you finally emerge from the bedroom for sustenance, he goes into the kitchen and complains that he can't find anything. Or maybe he starts moving things back to where they used to be. Just little things, but he keeps doing it. Two days later, he's getting on your last nerve.

Why is it so much harder to go to sleep with him in your bed now? You'd have thought you'd sleep like the dead with the comfort of his warm body next to you. And why do you have this urge to go along behind him and put things back where you think they should go? And why do you feel so resentful every time he questions you about why you did this or that, why you chose this thing over that thing?

As a member of a couple, we're used to making joint decisions. We get in the habit of discussing our ideas soon after they occur to us and getting the input of our mates very naturally before making changes. It isn't about getting permission or approval from him, it's just natural to discuss what's on your mind with your mate, or at least it is when you see him everyday.

Once your mate is living somewhere else though, no matter how closely you stay in contact, you don't have time to discuss every little thing. Slowly you adapt to more of a single person's way of making decisions, which is to mull over an idea and then maybe decide to give it a try. If you like the new way, you keep it. He's doing the same thing in his new place. But when he comes back home and you both start slipping into couple mode again, he looks at your changes and begins to approve or disapprove of them, retroactively. There you are, so proud of having handled it all on your own despite your misery at being without him, expecting him to be proud of you, too. And instead, if he doesn't like something you've done, suddenly you feel resentful towards him. He has no idea how hard it is to do everything alone, and he'd rather complain about where you've put the trash can than notice that you've taken care of every last thing that needed to be done, including getting the oil changed in the car. How dare he complain! If he wants to worry about that kind of thing, he can damn well stay here and take care of it himself!

Isn't it funny how easily you get angry over the sorts of problems that would be solved by him remaining at home? It's your brain's way of trying to rid you of your pain. The more urgent the problems begin to seem, the more likely it is that he will opt not to leave again. Hence the brain starts magnifying everything in an effort to achieve its goal, and thereby rid you of your emotional pain. It's all part of the self-preservation instinct at work, and proves we aren't really so far removed from our cave-person ancestors, no matter how much we might like to believe otherwise. The threat is emotional pain rather than wolves at the door, but the fight-or-flight response remains active and reliable.

Gary is a very easy-going, relaxed kind of guy, yet whenever he would return home for a visit, I always felt a bit encroached upon as though my space were being invaded. I wanted him there more than anything, yet it felt odd having him poking around the house, looking through things asking questions. For him, it was just a way of getting familiar and comfortable again, with the house and with us as a couple. But I felt that he was questioning my judgment, as though he didn't trust me to have taken care of everything and to have made good decisions in his absence.

The answer to this problem is just to know that it's coming, and to understand from his point of view, as well as your own, what's happening. You feel proud of yourself, but also a little bit insecure in your new role of Person Solely Responsible For Everything. So you might be just a little bit touchy. He feels superfluous, as though maybe, just maybe, you don't need him anymore. Looking through things and asking questions is his way of reconnecting to your life together, of feeling wanted and needed, of feeling as though he belongs there. If you keep in mind that he's engaging in male nesting behavior, watching him move the salt shaker from where you keep it to a far less convenient place on the other side of the kitchen, feels pretty endearing. After all, he's nesting with you.

♡♡♡

The Woman-to-Woman Bit. I know that sooner or later, probably in the middle of some interview, I am going to really regret writing this section. There is nothing I hate more than some man telling me that women behave irrationally due to their menstrual cycles. Hearing that makes me want to choke the life out of the guy saying it. And if I happen to hear it the day before my period starts... well, I've always managed to stop choking them in time.

As you are well aware, the vast majority of women do not become irrational, or lose their minds, or do anything else particularly dire in the days preceding the onset of their periods. Most of us do, however, feel things more deeply than we might otherwise. A sad movie is going to require a few more tissues just then, a friend you haven't seen in a while is going to get a longer, tighter hug, and a problem in your relationship is going to seem bigger than it ordinarily would.

The worst thing about it is that every woman with whom I've ever discussed this topic, myself included, is still taken by surprise every month when it happens. Invariably, I will be wondering why my life suddenly sucks so much long before it occurs to me that my period is due tomorrow. Several of my girlfriends and I have fallen into the habit of saying, "I'm not minimizing the problem in any way, okay? But when is your period due?" whenever one of us seems to be more upset than a problem really warrants. About ninety percent of the time the answer to that question is a long pause, followed by the "Damn!" that means, why the hell didn't I think of that? And then there's a bout of relieved laughter, and the realization that life doesn't really suck so much, or at least it won't by tomorrow.

I was getting frustrated one day because I couldn't find some things that I needed in order to do my work. It seemed that my things were spread out in all these different places and I felt so disorganized. I looked in my husband's home office and I thought how unfair it was that he has this nice space that he hardly ever uses and I work at home and don't even have an office. I just sit on the couch with my laptop and I have nowhere to put any of my things and it was just awful. I started to cry. Did you get that? I was crying because I didn't have a desk. I still laugh when I think about it. My period started the next day. I bought a desk. Problem solved.

Your feelings are valid no matter what prompts them. The only questions you need to ask yourself are when and if to act on them. If you're in tears over a problem, especially if it seems like things are just falling apart around you, my suggestion is to check the calendar before you take any action. If your period is due, give it all a day or two before you make any decisions. Then, if choking him is still the best solution, at least you'll know it was a cognitive decision rather than a hormonal one.

Who's Leaving, Who's Left Behind, and Why. On the surface separation is separation and you might not think it makes much difference which of you is leaving home, but it does have an effect on the types of pressures you each must endure. For example, the person leaving home is immersed in a whole new world. He has the advantage of never seeing the 'blank spaces' where you used to be, in that favorite cushy chair in the living room, in the passenger seat of his car, on your side of the bed. If you're the one left at home, every place you see, everything you touch reminds you of him because he's shared all those things with you. Everything you enjoyed together is empty once he's gone. On the other hand, the person left behind still has a support system and the comfort of friends and pets and a cozy nest to come home to, whereas the traveler has nothing familiar to cling to and misses not only you, but everything that means home to him.

If the traveler is going into a dangerous situation, such as the separations inherent in the lives of military families, or if he's leaving to go work on a drilling rig in the North Sea, the anxiety on both sides escalates tremendously. Every goodbye might be the last words you exchange and no matter how unspoken those fears are, they loom over you constantly. Even when the danger is small, love can make it overwhelming. I have waved goodbye to Gary at the airport at least a hundred times, but never once have I turned away without the thought crossing my mind that if that plane crashes, this is the last glimpse I'll have of him.

In an odd way, this part of the separation is easier on the person leaving, even if he is going into danger. He knows you're safe at home and that thought is comforting to him and makes the world seem a sane place. The best thing you can do for someone in this situation is be okay. He won't be if you're not, and the last thing you want is to risk putting him in further jeopardy by being a source of worry and distraction.

The difference between being the person who goes and being the person who stays, shows itself again during your visits. When Gary was working in Denver and I flew up there to spend a weekend with him, it was like a honeymoon. He'd clear his desk of work before I arrived, and the whole time I was there, it was just the two of us doing couple things all alone. It was, of course, bliss.

When he came home to Austin on the other hand, the visits weren't even close to being uninterrupted. He had a whole life in Austin before he left, with family and friends who missed him, and a house and car and bank accounts that needed attention. With each trip home only a weekend long, by the time he'd visited with his family and seen a few friends, paid the bills and run the errands, we were lucky if we managed a single evening all to ourselves.

Once again resentment reared its ugly head. Even though I understood perfectly well that he only had so much time to get everything done, and that in addition to missing me he missed being home, it was still hard not to feel abandoned while he was busy doing other things. After all, I'd paid my bills and visited my friends while he was away. For me, this time was reserved just for him.

The best thing to do is provide a safety net by planning a secondary activity for yourself and making sure it's available when he's home. Something as simple as having a good book on hand can spell the difference between the two of you sitting contentedly in a room together, each absorbed in a different activity, or you sulking miserably while he scrambles to balance his checkbook, with a cloud of guilt and budding resentment hanging in the air.

Keeping on good terms with his family and friends by generously sharing his time with them can pay off for you in other ways, as well. Your friends are probably sick of hearing you go on and on about how wonderful he is, but other people who love and miss him, such as his mother, will be happy to listen to you rhapsodize, and will likely join in with some stories of their own. If you're comfortable enough with his family and friends to spend time with them even when he's not around, you might find yourself with a wonderful support group to help you through the hard times.

Long-Distance Sex
(Oh, yes, Virginia...
there is such a thing!)

It's very much about pleasing the other person, just as real life sex is, but it requires a lot more creativity to describe a touch or a kiss in such a way that your mate actually feels it, and making him feel it is your goal.

♡♡♡

As I write this, I can't help wondering how many of you have skipped to this chapter first, because I probably would.

When you're madly in love, going for weeks or months at a stretch without any intimate contact is a big problem. If you're currently in a LDR, you don't need me to tell you how miserable it can be. No substitute is ever going to be even close to as good as the real thing, so don't get your hopes up, but when you're apart for a long time, virtual sex is still much better than no sex at all.

So what are your options? If you're like Gary and I were during the long-distance part of our relationship, you spend a lot of time fantasizing about making love to your sweetheart, which results in a certain amount of -- let's call it 'tension' -- and the only relief you get from all that tension is of the self-inflicted variety. Blush if you must, but you know it's true.

Learning to Say It. It is possible, however, to greatly improve the quality of the self-gratifying experience by sharing it with your lover, either on the phone, in a letter, or online. You might be a little shy about it at first because you'll be using words and phrases that one doesn't often use in the course of normal conversation, but there are huge benefits to getting past that shyness. Not only will it greatly enhance the excitement of those solo flights and make them much more satisfying for you and your partner, but learning to talk in a sexually explicit manner with your mate is one of the best things you can do to ensure that your sex life will still be exciting ten or twenty years down the road. There are couples who've been married and having sex for forty years and have never had the nerve to tell each other what they really want. Think of all the pleasure they've missed together. That's just sad, and it certainly doesn't have to be that way.

On the phone, in letters, or online, the closest you can get to having sex is talking about it, so you will eventually cover every detail of everything you've ever thought of or fantasized about. You'll peel back the top layer of those deep, dark desires and find still deeper ones to share, and so will he. When you and your mate are back together, your real life sex will be so much better as a result of these intimate conversations you've had on the subject. Trust me when I tell you that, even years later, you'll think back to those steamy conversations and be so glad that you had that time to get to know each other's wants and desires so well.

How to Have Sex, Virtually. So how does one have virtual sex, and, more importantly, how does one have good virtual sex? It can be an extremely creative and sensual experience. It's very much about pleasing the other person, just as real life sex is, but it requires a lot more creativity to describe a touch or a kiss in such a way that your mate actually feels it, and making him feel it is your goal. When done well, virtual sex will leave both of you with that same warm afterglow you normally enjoy together after sex.

I took a quick poll of people I know who are involved in long-distance relationships and who regularly have virtual sex with their mates. I asked them what makes it really good. Their comments included: be open, honest and sincere, give your vivid imagination free rein, trust your partner, allow yourself to feel very sensual, be detailed in your descriptions because you want your partner to really feel every caress in his mind, and most of all, be yourself.

In its interactive written form, such as in a chat room or when conversing online via an instant messaging system like ICQ, a virtual sexual scene is like a fantasy composed by two people together. One partner will describe something, then the other partner will describe his or her response to that and then add to it. For example, a scene might begin like this:

Him: Approaching you from behind, I brush your hair off your shoulder, exposing the smooth curve of your neck. Leaning forward... trailing teasing kisses from just below your ear to the sensitive curve of your shoulder... biting you gently there... feeling goosebumps form on your arms as I stroke them. Stepping closer still... pressing the length of my body to your back... wrapping my arms around your waist to pull you tight against me... my breath teasing your neck... your ear....

Her: Closing my eyes and leaning my head back over your shoulder... enjoying the feel of your lips against my neck, your hands stroking my arms... shivering in pleasure as I feel your teeth sinking into the tender curve of my neck, your arms sliding around my waist, your warm hard body pressed tightly to mine from behind. Arms at my sides, reaching back, I drag my fingernails up the outsides of your thighs, feeling your muscles bunch under my hands as I do so....

It really just amounts to you fantasizing what he describes and vice versa. Think about what you'd like to do if he suddenly appeared in front of you, then describe it in loving detail. When you respond to a passage from your mate, read it slowly, imagine it happening, and allow yourself to feel it. Then simply describe what you would do if he were really doing those things to you at this moment. Be honest and open, leaving nothing out. The things that you might want to shy away from writing or admitting out loud are likely the very things that will most inflame his senses, so don't hold back. Use language you would have a hard time using in real life. You'll be surprised at how exciting it can be for both of you.

Don't be surprised if you feel a bit awkward the first time. It's quite normal to be nervous and maybe have a case of stage fright. Try to keep it all very casual, just letting the normal conversation drift in a sexy direction, letting it build heat as it goes along. If you enjoy a glass of wine or a beer, this might be a good time to indulge yourself a little, just to take the edge off your inhibitions. Be careful though if you're online and have to write. Drink enough to relax a bit, but not so much that you lose the ability to type coherently.

Where's the Virtual Bedroom? You can have these virtual dates in private chat rooms, through private conversations in public chat rooms, or by using instant messaging systems like ICQ. It builds intimacy, improves communication skills, promotes creativity, clarifies your sexual needs to your partner and his to you, it's a lot of fun, and if you use an ISP

(Internet service provider) that offers unlimited hours, you can stay as long as you like and it doesn't cost a thing.

If you don't have a place where you like to chat, or your normal chat room has restrictions on the language you can use, even in private, just do a search on the word 'chat' and try out some new places until you find one you like. More and more adult-oriented chat sites, such as ChAtlantis (http://www.chatlantis.com), are springing up and those are especially friendly toward explicit conversation.

The instant messaging systems that are available now may offer the most privacy of all, since they allow you to initiate a private chat just between the two of you, completely eliminating the risk that you might accidentally post a private message publicly. If you don't currently use an instant messaging system, ask your friends what they use and give it a try. Most are available free and just have to be downloaded.

Aural Sex. The only sex substitute better than virtual sex is aural sex, and Gary and I had the phone bills to prove it! The basics of how it works are the same as virtual sex, with you each describing in detail what you would do to and with one another if you were together at that moment. The differences are in the immediacy of the experience. There's no waiting for that passage to be typed and sent. Holding a phone is a lot easier than typing and only requires one hand (ahem!). But best of all is the thrill of hearing the voice of your love. Listening to the way his breathing changes when you say certain things, the way his voice deepens and slows when he describes removing your clothing, piece by piece, truly is the next best thing to being there. No matter how sexy you find his voice, you don't appreciate it in person nearly as much as you will over the phone, especially in intimate conversation, simply because in person you have the whole rest of him distracting you. On the phone your entire attention is focused on his voice, and you'll hear every nuance, every breath. If you've never aroused your lover on the phone before, I can only say, go call him! Now!

The Erotic Vignette. If all of this is just a bit too much for you, you might prefer to write your love a sexy story and e-mail or post it to him. It's a bit easier in that you can take your time and enjoy your privacy while you write it, and it has the advantage of being there for reading over and over again. When Gary and I were dating, we used to write each other normal letters and enclose a second sealed envelope containing a sexy letter. It was very exciting to get the mail and open the letter and enjoy it, and then to tuck that second envelope away for reading in the evening, when I was home alone and all snug in bed for the night. I tended to have a little Mona Lisa smile all day when I knew I had one of those letters waiting for me at home. And now, six years later, we still have all those letters and every once in a while, we get them out and read them to each other. (The thought of which has, once again, given me that little Mona Lisa smile.)

In my opinion, the best method to use for that is the he/she third person sort of writing. Imagine that you are outside yourself, watching your lover and yourself together, and describe what you see. Be sure and start a new paragraph each time you change from describing the responses of one person to describing those of the other.

"He pushed her back against the wall, lifting her wrists and pinning them on either side of her head with his hands, his gaze flickering from her

eyes to her trembling lips. The expression on his face softened as he leaned in, taking her mouth with his, his tongue sliding hotly between her parted lips.

Gasping into his mouth at the first touch of his lips, she tried to fight it, still angry at him, but his kiss melted her resistance and set her knees to trembling. Her body swayed irresistibly toward him, her breasts pressing into his chest, her lips parted for him in open invitation."

Examples of this type of writing are easy to find in any romance novel. They aren't called bodice rippers for nothing, you know. Just remember that you're writing for a man, so use graphic terminology and avoid excessive use of the flowery phrase.

That Little Extra Feeling of Security. In a long-distance relationship it's almost impossible to completely eliminate the worry that your man is going to become sexually involved with someone else, someone there and attainable, unlike you sitting hundreds or thousands of miles away where he can't reach you. Even if you're sure he's not the kind of guy who'd cheat, the sheer pressure of knowing that he's going so long without any sexual activity will make you feel a little insecure. None of the methods that I have described are as satisfying as a real sexual relationship, of course, but they still give you the opportunity to satisfy each other's needs for intimacy and for sexual expression, at least enough to make it easier to remain faithful to one another. You'll find yourself planning little seductive scenarios and acting them out, and that will keep your sexual energy focused completely on one another, giving you both that extra measure of security that comes from knowing that you're still taking care of each other, despite the distance between you. Besides, it's so much fun!

The Light at the End of the Tunnel

*When you've walked through fire, you know
in your heart that you can do anything.*

For all the hardship that you're enduring now, you have amazing rewards to look forward to in the future. Being in love and living apart forces two people to learn to express their needs, wants, desires, thoughts, and feelings to a degree that most people never do. You will always have that. It's a strength that can't be bought, and is only earned through loving each other enough to work for it. Treasure it. There is no knowledge or skill of greater value.

By remaining faithful to one another, despite the distance and the time, you're showing each other that it's safe to trust. As you each see the other remain true, you're developing a deeper level of mutual respect than most couples ever have. In sticking together through these hard times, you're proving the strength of your commitment to one another, enabling you to feel secure in your love. By working out whatever difficulties you encounter and problems that arise, you're opening lines of communication that will enrich your lives every day. You're learning how to set realistic expectations that will spare you disappointment, and how to compromise to meet all your needs. You're both growing as individuals, in ways you might never have without this challenge. You are learning to give more than you ever have, and you're getting more in return.

During this time, the two of you are growing emotional, mental, and spiritual bonds that will sustain you through anything you will ever face in the future. There will be nothing that you can't handle together.

In the four-day seminars given by the motivational speaker, Anthony Robbins, the attendees walk barefooted across a bed of hot coals on the very first night. He teaches them everything they need to know to get through it successfully, then sends them out to do it. It seems a lot to ask of people on day one, but he does it to prove a point. When you've walked through fire, you know in your heart that you can do anything.

Most relationships don't have to endure the kind of pressure that long-distance relationships do. That seems like a good thing, and if all that mattered was keeping every relationship intact for as long as possible, it would be. But in the real world, no relationship skates along forever without some kind of pressure. Eventually they are all put to the test. It might be three years down the road when a couple decides to have their first child, or five years into it when one person loses a job and can't find another, or ten years later when someone has an affair. But it always happens sooner or later. Many relationships won't survive those tests.

Right now, you're walking through fire. You know everything you need to know to bring your relationship through it in good shape. And when you've done it, and this time apart is over, you will both know in your hearts that you can do anything… together.

- Kimberli Bryan

P.S. You can mail me or Stephen Blake directly through Anton Publishing's website at www.sblake.com, or write to us at:

Anton Publishing
305 Madison Ave.
Suite 1166
New York, New York 10165.

It's only when you stop dismissing miracles as coincidence that you find your destiny.

Order Loving Your Long-Distance Relationship, Still Loving, or Loving Your Long-Distance Relationship for Women.

To order, send this page along with a check or money order for $6.99 U.S. or $9.99 Canadian each plus $2. shipping and handling for one copy, 50¢ shipping and handling for each additional copy, to:

Anton Publishing
305 Madison Ave
Suite 1166
New York, New York 10165

Book Title(s) _____

Name _____

Address _____

City _____ State/Province _____

Zip/Postal Code _____